Lewis Hamilton

by

Andy Croft

Illustrated by Dylan Gibson

First published in 2010 in Great Britain by
Barrington Stoke Ltd
18 Walker St, Edinburgh, EH3 7LP

www.barringtonstoke.co.uk

ISBN: 978-1-84299-751-2

Printed in Great Britain by Bell & Bain Ltd

A Note from the Author

I used to think that Formula 1 was boring. What's so exciting about a lot of cars going round and round a track? Anyway, cars win races, not drivers.

Then Lewis Hamilton came along. Young, black and British. And a winner. Like a lot of people, I started watching Formula 1 because of Lewis Hamilton.

While I was writing this book I was also writing a book about the boxer Amir Khan. They are both stories about ordinary kids who have done extraordinary things. And they are both stories about hard work and sticking to one's dream.

Not everyone can do as well as Lewis Hamilton. Or be as cool. But everyone can try.

Contents

Contents

Chapter 1

World Champion

The date is 2nd November 2008. It's a hot, wet day in Brazil. Tens of thousands of people are here for the Brazil Grand Prix.

It's the last race of the season. Everyone is watching the young British driver Lewis Hamilton. It's only his second year as a

Formula 1 driver. He's only 23. But he's hoping to become the World Champion today. Can he do it?

Only one man can stop him. The Brazilian driver, Felipe Massa. The local crowd want Massa to win. But Lewis Hamilton only needs to finish 5th to be the World Champion.

Massa starts in pole position at the front. Lewis Hamilton is in 4th position just behind him. The rain is making the track slippy. And unsafe. The cars are ready. The drivers

are ready. The crowd is ready. And they're off!

As they go into the first corner, Lewis Hamilton is just three cars behind Massa. But by lap 11 he has slipped to 6th place. He pulls back into 5th place. But the German driver Vettel is close behind. On lap 69 it starts raining. Lewis Hamilton goes wide and Vettel shoots past him into 5th place.

As Massa crosses the finish line to win the race he thinks he has also won the title. His team starts to celebrate. But Lewis

Hamilton won't give up. He and Vettel are on the last lap. Suddenly, on the last corner Lewis Hamilton pulls into 5th place. He crosses the line. He has done it!

Lewis Hamilton is Formula 1 World Champion.

He's the youngest driver ever to win the title.

He's also the first black driver to win it.

This is his story.

Chapter 2

Behind the Wheel

Lewis Carl Hamilton was born in Stevenage, north of London, on the 7th of January 1985. He was named after the famous black American sprinter Carl Lewis.

His grandparents moved to Britain in the 1950s from Grenada in the West Indies. His granddad worked on the London Underground. His dad worked for British Rail. His mum worked for the local council.

When Lewis was only two, his mum and dad split up. Lewis lived with his mum and his older half-sisters Nikky and Sam. His dad lived not far away. When his mum moved to London, Lewis went to live with his dad, his step-mother Linda and his half-brother Nico.

Lewis went to the local primary school and then to John Henry Newman Secondary School. He played football for the school team (England and Aston Villa star Ashley Young played in the same team). He was also in the cricket, basketball and athletics teams.

When Lewis was five, his dad bought him a little remote control car for his birthday. He used to race it round the house. A few months later his dad made him a bigger remote control car. They joined a local club for remote control car fans. Soon Lewis was racing against grown-ups. And winning!

He came 2nd in the club championship and 2nd in the national BRCA championship

the following year. Lewis did so well he was asked to be on *Blue Peter*!

Two years later his dad bought him a very special Christmas present. It was wrapped. But Lewis knew what it was. A second-hand go-kart ...

Chapter 3

Karting

Lewis started kart racing when he was only eight. He began in the Cadet class. Soon he was winning all the races. Some of the other parents didn't like this. They told him to back off. So he started learning karate. So did his dad.

By the time Lewis was ten, he was the Super 1 Series champion and Superprix champion.

That year Lewis met the McLaren racing boss Ron Dennis. "I want to race for you one day," he said. Dennis wrote in his autograph book, "Phone me in nine years, we'll sort something out then." But Lewis didn't have to wait until he was 19 to drive for McLaren.

The next year he won the McLaren Mercedes Champions of the Future, the UK 5 Nations and the Kart Masters Championship.

The following season he raced in the Junior Yamaha section. He won the Champions of the Future series, and was Super One series British champion.

He was so good he was on *Blue Peter* again!

By 1998 he was racing in the Junior Intercontinental A section. He finished 4th in the Italian Open Championship and 2nd in the McLaren Mercedes Champions of the Future. His prize was a trip to the Belgian Grand Prix. There he met Ron Dennis again.

Dennis knew this young boy would go far. He asked him to join McLaren. Lewis was still only 13. He was the youngest driver ever to be taken on by a Formula 1 team.

In 1999 he was Italian Champion and Vice European Champion.

The next year he was driving in Formula A. He was the European Champion, World Cup champion and ranked number one in the Champion Kart driver ratings.

It was time to move up a gear.

Chapter 4

Formula Racing

Lewis Hamilton began his car racing career in the 2001 British Formula Renault Winter Series. He was only 16.

His first test-drive in a racing car didn't go very well. He had never driven a real car before and he crashed it after three laps. But

it wasn't long before he was showing once again how good he was. He finished 5th in the winter series.

The next year he finished 3rd in Formula Renault with three wins. The boy was learning fast. The next year he won the championship with 10 wins, nine fastest laps and 419 points. The next best racing driver only won two races.

Where next for Lewis Hamilton? Formula 3.

Chapter 5

Formula 3

Lewis Hamilton's Formula 3 career started badly. He was forced out of his first race with a flat tyre. He crashed in his second race and had to be taken to hospital.

But he showed his speed at the Macau and the Korean Grand Prix. At the end of the

2004 Formula 3 European series he was 5th overall. That year he won the Bahrain Formula 3 Superprix. He was only 20.

The next season, 2005, Lewis Hamilton won 15 out of 20 races with 10 fastest laps. Champion again. That year he won the Formula 3 Masters.

After only two seasons in Formula 3, Lewis Hamilton was ready for the next stage. Grand Prix 2. This is the level below Formula 1.

Chapter 6
Grand Prix 2

It was only Lewis Hamilton's first season in Grand Prix 2. But he soon made a name for himself. He won two races in Germany. He won in Monte-Carlo. He won both races at Silverstone. He even overtook on a bend at 150mph. In Turkey he came back from a bad spin to finish in 2nd place.

At the end of the season Lewis Hamilton was champion again with five wins and six fastest laps. Next stop – Formula 1.

Ron Dennis was now looking for a new driver for the Mclaren Formula 1 team. Juan Pablo Montoya and Kimi Räikkönen had just left. McLaren needed a new team-mate for Fernando Alonso. Ron Dennis knew which driver he wanted.

Lewis Hamilton was ready for Formula 1. But was Formula 1 ready for Lewis Hamilton?

Chapter 7

Formula 1

Lewis Hamilton got off to a flying start in the 2007 Formula 1 season. He finished 3rd in his first race. He finished 2nd in Malaysia, Bahrain, Spain and Monaco. After only five races he was leading the drivers' championship!

He won the Canadian Grand Prix. He won the US Grand Prix. He came 3rd in the French Grand Prix. Lewis Hamilton was now 14 points ahead of any other driver.

The next race was the British Grand Prix at Silverstone. The stands were packed. Everyone wanted to see their new British hero. Hamilton drove the fastest time in practice. He led for the first 16 laps. But then he slipped to 3rd, 40 seconds behind Räikkönen and Alonso.

During a practice session for the European Grand Prix, he crashed after a

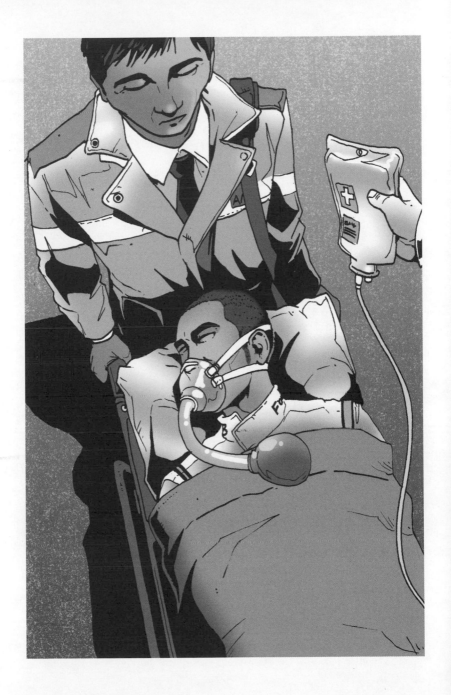

problem with a wheel nut. He was taken to the medical centre on a stretcher with an oxygen mask and drip.

He won the Hungarian Grand Prix. But when he had a flat tyre in Turkey he had to drive slowly back to the pits and he only finished 5th. He was 4th in the Belgian Grand Prix. He won the Japanese Grand Prix in heavy rain. With only two races left Lewis Hamilton was still 12 points ahead. Could he win the championship in his first season?

At the Chinese Grand Prix the track was wet, so he was driving with his wet-tyres on the car. When the sun came out his tyres began to wear out. He took a pit-stop to change his tyres. But as he pulled into the pit lane his back-brakes wouldn't work. He skidded off the track. Race over. He was gutted.

Now he was only four points ahead of Alonso and seven points ahead of Räikkönen. The last race of the season was the Brazilian Grand Prix. Massa started in front. Hamilton started in second place. But then

Räikkönen passed him on the outside. At the third corner, Alonso passed him on the inside. Hamilton's brakes locked and he went off the track. By the time he was back in the race he was in 8th place.

Hamilton did his best to catch up with the leaders. By the next lap he was in 7th place. Soon he was in 6th place. But then he had a problem with his gear-box. He couldn't change gear. He had to slow down while he reset the car's computer. By now he was in 18th place. But he wouldn't give up.

He started to overtake, first one car then another. By lap 15, he had climbed to 11th place. By lap 59 he was up to 8th. Just 12 laps to go. On the last lap Hamilton was in 7th place. But it just wasn't good enough. Räikkönen won the race and the championship. He had 110 points. Hamilton and Alonso each had 109 points.

Lewis Hamilton was frustrated. So were his fans. But the next season was only a few months away ...

Chapter 8
Number 1

In January 2008, Lewis Hamilton signed a multi-million pound contract to stay with McLaren-Mercedes until the end of 2012.

He won the first race of 2008 in Melbourne. He finished 5th in Malaysia. At the Bahrain Grand Prix he crashed into the back of Alonso and only finished in 13th place.

But he was 3rd in Spain and 2nd in Turkey. Two weeks later, he won the Monaco Grand Prix. This meant that Lewis Hamilton was top of the drivers' championship again.

At the Canadian Grand Prix, the drivers had to wait in the pit lane while a broken car was moved off the track. Räikkönen was waiting at the end of the pit lane at a red light. Lewis Hamilton was in a hurry to get back into the race. He didn't see the red

light and he smashed into the back of Räikkönen's car. Both cars were wrecked and were out of the race.

It was raining heavily during the British Grand Prix at Silverstone. There was a lot of spray everywhere. All the other cars were spinning on the wet track. Only Lewis Hamilton had the skill to stay on the track and to win the race.

He won again in Germany by nine seconds. Then he won the Belgian Grand Prix. But he was given a 25 second penalty for passing Kimi Räikkönen after cutting a corner. So he only finished 3rd. At the Italian Grand Prix he was 7th. His lead was down to one point.

Lewis Hamilton finished 3rd in Singapore. But then things went very wrong in Japan. He started slowly. Then Räikkönen took the lead. Lewis Hamilton tried to overtake on the first corner, but he braked too late and went wide. Then Massa crashed into him and put him into a spin. By the time he came out of the spin he was last but one. He pulled back but he could only finish 12th.

A win in China put him seven points ahead of Massa. There was only one race left.

The date is 2nd November 2008. It's a hot day in Brazil. Tens of thousands of people are here for the Brazil Grand Prix ...

The rest is history. The rest is legend. The legend of Lewis Hamilton.

Chapter 9

Life in the Fast Lane

Lewis Hamilton is now a sporting super-star. He has millions of fans all over the world. Everyone wants his autograph. Everyone wants his photo. In 2009 he was given an award, the MBE, by the Queen when he was still only 24.

He travels all round the world. During the Formula 1 season he races in 18 different countries. That's a different country every two weeks. He advertises cars, watches, sports-wear, mobile-phones and a bank. He earns nearly £100 million a year.

He is friends with hip-hop stars Pharrel Williams and P Diddy. He used to go out with Miss World. At the moment his girlfriend is Nicole Scherzinger from the Pussycat Dolls. But Lewis Hamilton is also a very private person who wants a life of his own. He likes being away from the crowds and the cameras. Not long ago he moved to Switzerland, just to get away from all the photographers.

When he is not racing he spends as much time as he can with his friends and with his family. His family is very important to him. He visits his granddad in Grenada every year. He still likes going to the cinema, eating take-aways, playing computer games with his half-brother Nico. He still supports Arsenal.

He enjoys playing guitar, football, squash and tennis. He likes hip-hop, R&B, reggae and funky house. His favourite artists are The Roots, De La Soul, 2Pac, Bob Marley, Sizzla, Sean Paul and UB40.

His heroes are his dad, Muhammad Ali, Nelson Mandela and Martin Luther King. He is proud to be the first black Formula 1 champion. "Being black is not a negative," he says. "It's a positive, if anything, because I'm different."

And Lewis Hamilton is certainly different.

He is the best.

Barrington Stoke would like to thank all its readers for commenting on the manuscript before publication and in particular:

Lauren Crocker
T. Cutts
Alex Dall
Harrison Date
Connor Doyle
Abbey Finney
Ruth Garbett
Andrea Green
David Green

Laura Jordon
Danielle Jory
Jack Josephine
Soloman Matthews
Justin Moore
Diana Osborn
Charlotte Parnell
Liam Vickery
Jordan Wilkes

Become a Consultant!

Would you like to be a consultant? Ask your parent, carer or teacher to contact us at the email address below – we'd love to hear from them! They can also find out more by visiting our website.

schools@barringtonstoke.co.uk
www.barringtonstoke.co.uk

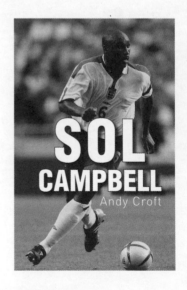

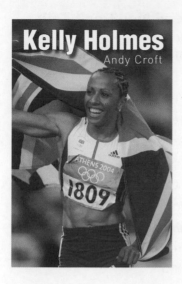

**Kelly Holmes
by
Andy Croft**

From
Defeat
Depression...

To gold medals!
Find out how Kelly Holmes
became an Olympic hero.

**Come On, Danny!
by
Andy Croft**

Danny's dad is in prison.
His teachers are on his
case.
His friends are on his back.
Can he find a way out?

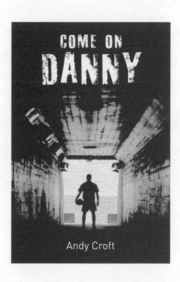

You can order these books directly from our website at
www.barringtonstoke.co.uk

Alien: Betrayal
by
Tony Bradman

The second Alien adventure – the war goes on.
Jake has been betrayed.
And it was someone in his squad.
Can he find out who it was?

Alligator
by
Theresa Breslin

Jono has a problem.
He's just got himself an alligator.
His mum is going to kill him.
Unless the alligator gets there first ...

You can order these books directly from our website at
www.barringtonstoke.co.uk